THE BOOTLEG SERIES **Vol. 9**

BOB DYLAN

THE WITMARK DEMOS:
1962-1964

Amsco Publications
A Part of **The Music Sales Group**
New York/London/Paris/Sydney/Copenhagen/Berlin/Tokyo/Madrid

Publishing Note: Contained herein are all of the known Witmark recordings. They include an unusual anomaly for a publisher. The song, "Baby, Let Me Follow You Down," is one that has existed in the folk tradition since the turn of the century. However, on the recorded introduction to the song on Bob Dylan's first album, he credits learning the song from Eric Von Schmidt. At the time, Von Schmidt declined copyrighting it as an arrangement of a public domain song. Towards the mid-seventies, Eric changed his mind and shared the arrangement with Reverend Gary Davis and Dave Van Ronk. It is those performers who now hold the copyright to this particular arrangement. We added it to make this collection complete.

Cover design and layout by Geoff Gans
Front cover photo by Douglas R. Gilbert
Back cover photo by John Cohen
Interior photography courtesy of The Sony Archive

This book Copyright © 2010 Special Rider Music.
Published 2010 by Amsco Publications,
A Division of Music Sales Corporation, New York

All rights reserved. No part of this book may be
reproduced in any form or by any electronic or mechanical means,
including information storage and retrieval systems,
without permission in writing from the publisher.

Order No. AM1002188
International Standard Book Number: 978.0.8256.3761.2
HL Item Number: 14041325

Exclusive Distributor for the United States, Canada, Mexico and U.S. possessions:
Hal Leonard Corporation
7777 West Bluemound Road, Milwaukee, WI 53213 USA

Exclusive Distributors for the rest of the World:
Music Sales Limited
14-15 Berners Street, London W1T 3LJ England
Music Sales Pty. Limited
20 Resolution Drive, Caringbah, NSW 2229, Australia

Printed in the United States of America by
Vicks Lithograph and Printing Corporation

CONTENTS

Man On The Street (Fragment)

Words and Music by Bob Dylan

Copyright © 1962 SONGS OF UNIVERSAL, INC. Copyright Renewed.
This arrangement Copyright © 2010 SONGS OF UNIVERSAL, INC.
All Rights Reserved. Used by Permission.
Reprinted by permission of Hal Leonard Corporation

Hard Times In New York Town

Words and Music by Bob Dylan

Guitar:
capo 2nd fret

Moderately fast

1. Come you la - dies and you gent - le - men, a - lis - ten to my song

Sing it to you right, but you might think it's wrong

Just a lit - tle glimpse of a sto - ry I'll tell 'Bout an

East Coast cit - y that you all know well___ It's hard___

___ times in the cit - y___ Liv - in' down in New York

town

1. - 6.

7.

2. Old

Copyright © 1962 SONGS OF UNIVERSAL, INC. Copyright Renewed.
This arrangement Copyright © 2010 SONGS OF UNIVERSAL, INC.
All Rights Reserved. Used by Permission.
Reprinted by permission of Hal Leonard Corporation

Additional lyrics

2. Old New York City is a friendly old town
   From Washington Heights to Harlem on down
   There's a-mighty many people all millin' all around
   They'll kick you when you're up and knock you when you're down
   It's hard times in the city
   Livin' down in New York town

3. It's a mighty long ways from the Golden Gate
   To Rockefeller Plaza 'n' the Empire State
   Mister Rockefeller sets up as high as a bird
   Old Mister Empire never says a word
   It's hard times from the country
   Livin' down in New York town

4. Well, it's up in the mornin' tryin' to find a job of work
   Stand in one place till your feet begin to hurt
   If you got a lot o' money you can make yourself merry
   If you only got a nickel, it's the Staten Island Ferry
   And it's hard times in the city
   Livin' down in New York town

5. Mister Hudson come a-sailin' down the stream
   And old Mister Minuet paid for his dream
   Bought your city on a one-way track
   'F I had my way I'd sell it right back
   And it's hard times in the city
   Livin' down in New York town

6. I'll take all the smog in Cal-i-for-ne-ay
   'N' every bit of dust in the Oklahoma plains
   'N' the dirt in the caves of the Rocky Mountain mines
   It's all much cleaner than the New York kind
   And it's hard times in the city
   Livin' down in New York town

7. So all you newsy people, spread the news around
   You c'n listen to m' story, listen to m' song
   You c'n step on my name, you c'n try 'n' get me beat
   When I leave New York, I'll be standin' on my feet
   And it's hard times in the city
   Livin' down in New York town

Poor Boy Blues

Words and Music by Bob Dylan

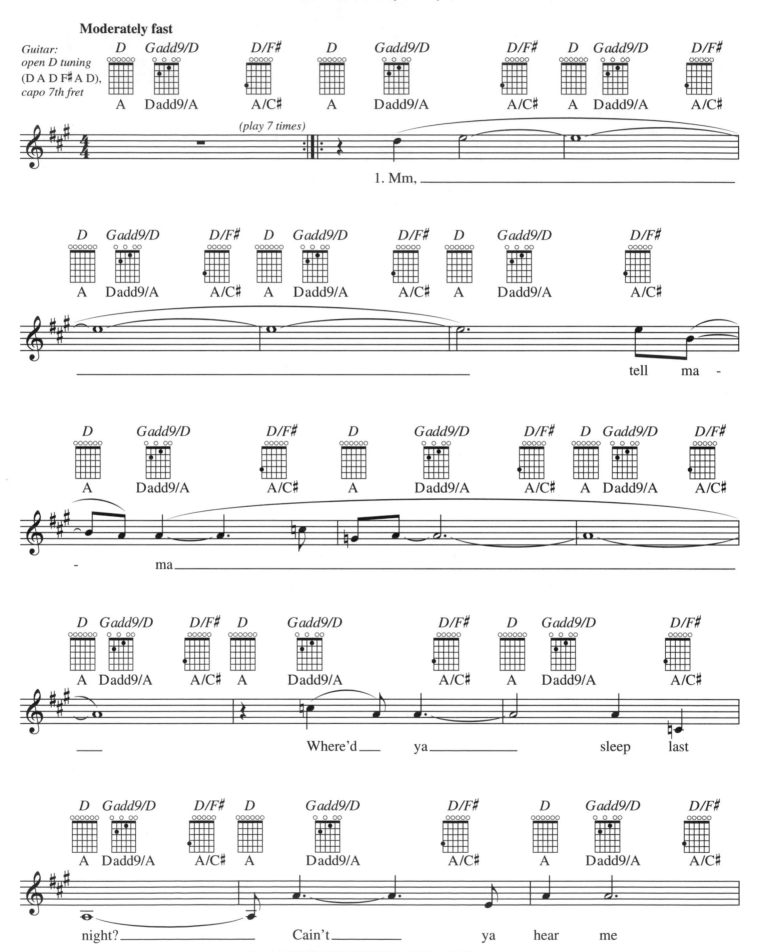

Copyright © 1962 SONGS OF UNIVERSAL, INC. Copyright Renewed.
This arrangement Copyright © 2010 SONGS OF UNIVERSAL, INC.
All Rights Reserved. Used by Permission.
Reprinted by permission of Hal Leonard Corporation

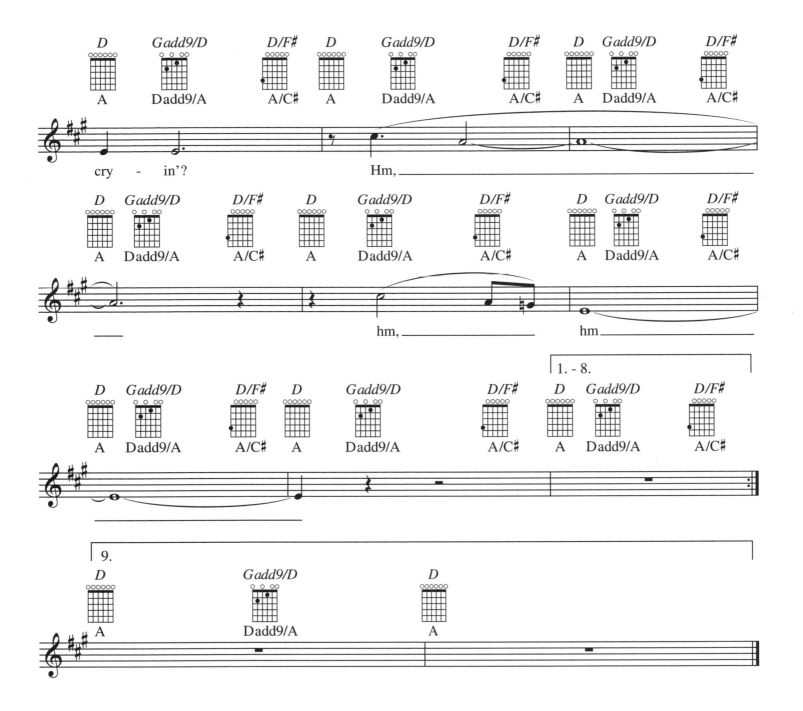

cry - in'?   Hm,

_____   hm,   hm

1. - 8.

9.

Additional lyrics

2. Hey, tell me baby
   What's the matter here?
   Cain't ya hear me cryin'?
   Hm, hm, hm

3. Hey, stop, you ol' train
   Let a poor boy ride
   Cain't ya hear me cryin'?
   Hm, hm, hm

4. Hey, Mister Bartender
   I swear I'm not too young
   Cain't ya hear me cryin'?
   Hm, hm, hm

5. Blow your whistle, policeman
   My poor feet are trained to run
   Cain't ya hear me cryin'?
   Hm, hm, hm

6. Long-distance operator
   I hear this phone call is on the house
   Cain't ya hear me cryin'?
   Hm, hm, hm

7. Ashes and diamonds
   The diff'rence I cain't see
   Cain't ya hear me cryin'?
   Hm, hm, hm

8. Mister Judge and Jury
   Cain't you see the shape I'm in?
   Don't ya hear me cryin'?
   Hm, hm, hm

9. Mississippi River
   You a-runnin' too fast for me
   Cain't ya hear me cryin'?
   Hm, hm, hm

Ballad For A Friend

Words and Music by Bob Dylan

Additional lyrics

2. Years ago we hung around
   Watchin' trains roll through the town
   Now that train is a-graveyard bound

3. Where we go up in that North Country
   Lakes and streams and mines so free
   I had no better friend than he

4. Something happened to him that day
   I thought I heard a stranger say
   I hung my head and stole away

5. A diesel truck was rollin' slow
   Pullin' down a heavy load
   And it left him on a Utah road

6. They carried him back to his home town
   His mother cried, his sister moaned
   Listenin' to them church bells tone

Copyright © 1962 SONGS OF UNIVERSAL, INC. Copyright Renewed.
This arrangement Copyright © 2010 SONGS OF UNIVERSAL, INC.
All Rights Reserved. Used by Permission.
Reprinted by permission of Hal Leonard Corporation

Man On The Street

Words and Music by Bob Dylan

Moderately

1. I'll sing_____ you a song, ain't_____ ver - y long

'Bout an old man who nev - er done wrong

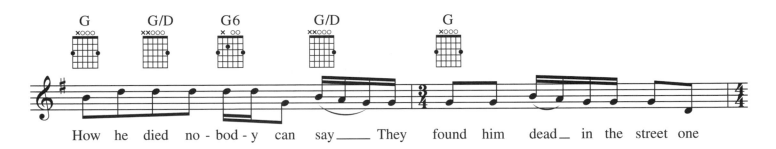

How he died no - bod - y can say_____ They found him dead_ in the street one

1. - 4. day 2. Well, the crowd,_ day **5.**

Additional lyrics

2. Well, the crowd, they gathered one fine morn
   At the man whose clothes 'n' shoes were torn
   There on the sidewalk he did lay
   They stopped 'n' stared 'n' walked their way

3. Well, the p'liceman come and he looked around
   "Get up, old man, or I'm a-takin' you down"
   He jabbed him once with his billy club
   And the old man then rolled off the curb

4. Well, he jabbed him again and loudly said
   "Call the wagon; this man is dead"
   The wagon come, they loaded him in
   I never saw the man again

5. I've sung you my song, it ain't very long
   'Bout an old man who never done wrong
   How he died no one can say
   They found him dead in the street one day

Copyright © 1962 SONGS OF UNIVERSAL, INC. Copyright Renewed.
This arrangement Copyright © 2010 SONGS OF UNIVERSAL, INC.
All Rights Reserved. Used by Permission.
Reprinted by permission of Hal Leonard Corporation

Rambling, Gambling Willie

Words and Music by Bob Dylan

Copyright © 1962 SONGS OF UNIVERSAL, INC. Copyright Renewed.
This arrangement Copyright © 2010 SONGS OF UNIVERSAL, INC.
All Rights Reserved. Used by Permission.
Reprinted by permission of Hal Leonard Corporation

Additional lyrics

2. He gambled in the White House and in the railroad yards
   Wherever there was people, there was Willie and his cards
   He had the reputation as the gamblin'est man around
   Wives would keep their husbands home when Willie came to town
   And it's ride, Willie, ride
   Roll, Willie, roll
   Wherever you are a-gamblin' now, nobody really knows

3. Sailin' down the Mississippi to a town called New Orleans
   They're still talkin' about their card game on that Jackson River Queen
   "I've come to win some money," Gamblin' Willie says
   When the game finally ended up, the whole damn boat was his
   And it's ride, Willie, ride
   Roll, Willie, roll
   Wherever you are a-gamblin' now, nobody really knows

4. Up in the Rocky Mountains in a town called Cripple Creek
   There was an all-night poker game, lasted about a week
   Nine hundred miners had laid their money down
   When Willie finally left the room, he owned the whole damn town
   And it's ride, Willie, ride
   Roll, Willie, roll
   Wherever you are a-gamblin' now, nobody really knows

5. But Willie had a heart of gold and this I know is true
   He supported all his children and all their mothers too
   He wore no rings or fancy things, like other gamblers wore
   He spread his money far and wide, to help the sick and the poor
   And it's ride, Willie, ride
   Roll, Willie, roll
   Wherever you are a-gamblin' now, nobody really knows

6. When you played your cards with Willie, you never really knew
   Whether he was bluffin' or whether he was true
   He won a fortune from a man who folded in his chair
   The man, he left a diamond flush, Willie didn't even have a pair
   And it's ride, Willie, ride
   Roll, Willie, roll
   Wherever you are a-gamblin' now, nobody really knows

7. It was late one evenin' during a poker game
   A man lost all his money, he said Willie was to blame
   He shot poor Willie through the head, which was a tragic fate
   When Willie's cards fell on the floor, they were aces backed with eights
   And it's ride, Willie, ride
   Roll, Willie, roll
   Wherever you are a-gamblin' now, nobody really knows

8. So all you rovin' gamblers, wherever you might be
   The moral of the story is very plain to see
   Make your money while you can, before you have to stop
   For when you pull that dead man's hand, your gamblin' days are up
   And it's ride, Willie, ride
   Roll, Willie, roll
   Wherever you are a-gamblin' now, nobody really knows

Talking Bear Mountain Picnic Massacre Blues

Words and Music by Bob Dylan

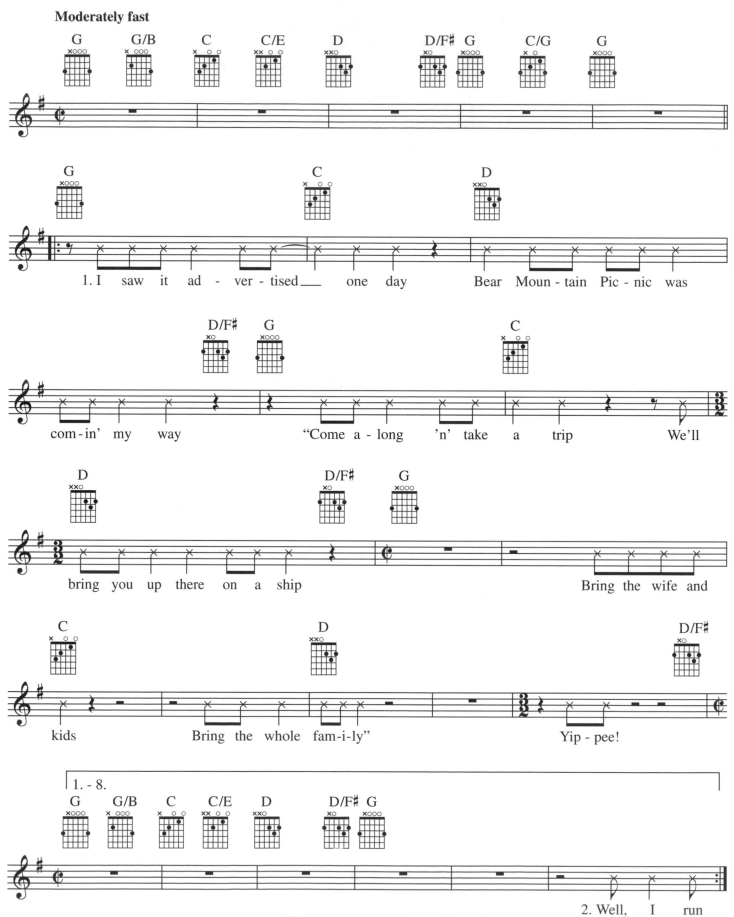

Copyright © 1962 SONGS OF UNIVERSAL, INC. Copyright Renewed.
This arrangement Copyright © 2010 SONGS OF UNIVERSAL, INC.
All Rights Reserved. Used by Permission.
Reprinted by permission of Hal Leonard Corporation

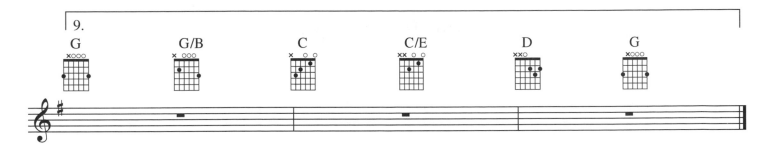

Additional lyrics

2. Well, I run right down 'n' bought a ticket
   To this Bear Mountain Picnic
   But little did I realize
   I was in for a picnic surprise
   Had nothin' to do with mountains
   I didn't even come close to a bear

3. Took the wife 'n' kids down to the pier
   Six thousand people there
   Everybody had a ticket for the trip
   "Oh well," I said, "it's a pretty big ship
   Besides, anyway, the more the merrier"

4. Well, we all got on 'n' what d'ya think
   That big old boat started t' sink
   More people kept a-pilin' on
   That old ship was a-slowly goin' down
   Funny way t' start a picnic

5. Well, I soon lost track of m' kids 'n' wife
   So many people there I never saw in m' life
   That old ship sinkin' down in the water
   Six thousand people tryin' t' kill each other
   Dogs a-barkin', cats a-meowin'
   Women screamin', fists a-flyin', babies cryin'
   Cops a-comin', me a-runnin'
   Maybe we just better call off the picnic

6. I got shoved down 'n' pushed around
   All I could hear there was a screamin' sound
   Don't remember one thing more
   Just remember wakin' up on a little shore
   Head busted, stomach cracked
   Feet splintered, I was bald, naked…
   Quite lucky to be alive though

7. Feelin' like I climbed outa m' casket
   I grabbed back hold of m' picnic basket
   Took the wife 'n' kids 'n' started home
   Wishin' I'd never got up that morn

8. Now, I don't care just what you do
   If you wanta have a picnic, that's up t' you
   But don't tell me about it, I don't wanta hear it
   'Cause, see, I just lost all m' picnic spirit
   Stay in m' kitchen, have m' own picnic…
   In the bathroom

9. Now, it don't seem to me quite so funny
   What some people are gonna do f'r money
   There's a bran' new gimmick every day
   Just t' take somebody's money away
   I think we oughta take some o' these people
   And put 'em on a boat, send 'em up to Bear Mountain…
   For a picnic

Standing On The Highway

Words and Music by Bob Dylan

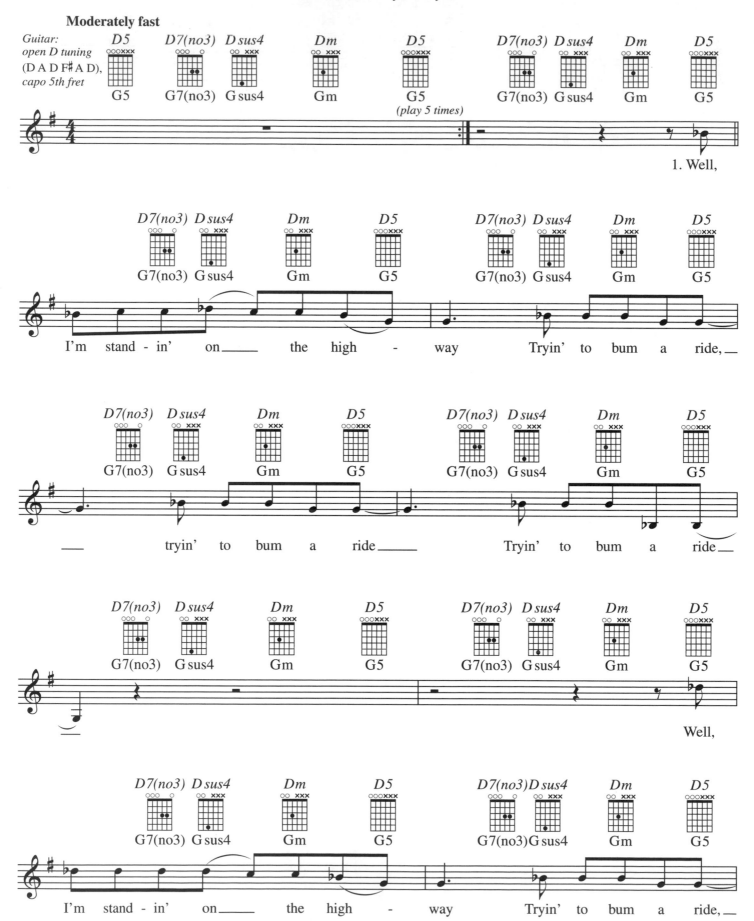

Copyright © 1962 SONGS OF UNIVERSAL, INC. Copyright Renewed.
This arrangement Copyright © 2010 SONGS OF UNIVERSAL, INC.
All Rights Reserved. Used by Permission.
Reprinted by permission of Hal Leonard Corporation

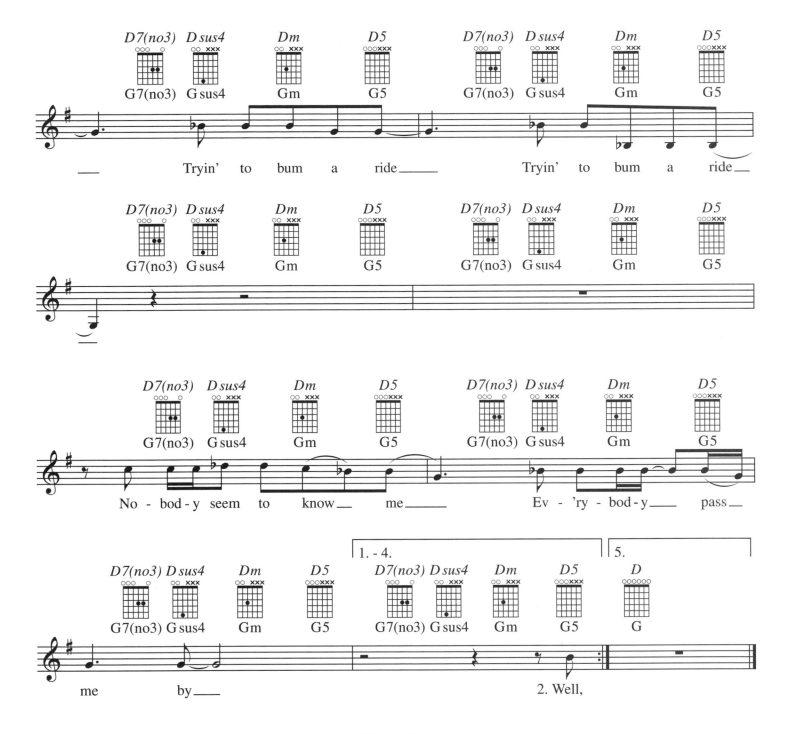

Additional lyrics

2. Well, I'm standin' on the highway
Tryin' to hold up, tryin' to hold up
Tryin' to hold up and be brave
Well, I'm standin' on the highway
Tryin' to hold up, tryin' to hold up and be brave
One road's goin' to the bright lights
The other's goin' down to my grave

3. Well, I'm standin' on the highway, vision clear
Well, I'm standin' on the highway, vision clear
Everybody passin' me by
Nobody seem to know I'm here

4. Well, I'm lookin' down at two cards
They seem to be handmade
Well, I'm lookin' down at two cards
They seem to be handmade
One looks like it's the ace of diamonds
The other looks like it is the ace of spades

5. Well, I'm standin' on the highway
Watchin' my life roll by
Well, I'm standin' on the highway
Watchin' my life roll by
Well, I'm standin' on the highway
Tryin' to bum a ride

Tomorrow Is A Long Time

Words and Music by Bob Dylan

* ad lib quasi recitative

Copyright © 1963 Warner Brothers Inc.; renewed 1991 Special Rider Music.
All Rights Reserved. International Copyright Secured.

BLOWIN' IN THE WIND

1. How many roads must a man walk down before he's called a man

   How many seas must the white dove sail before he sleeps in the sand

   How many times must the cannonballs fly before theyre forever banned

   The answer my friend is blowin' in the wind

   The answer is blowin' in the wind   Cho.

2. How many years can a mountain exist before it is washed to the sea

   How many years can some people exist before they're allowed to be free

   How many times can a man turn his head and pretend he just doesn't see

   Cho.

3. How many times must a man look up before he can see the sky

   How many ears must one man have before he can hear people cry

   How many deaths will it take til he knows that too many people have died

   CHO.

© 1962 Bob Dylan

Blowin' In The Wind

Words and Music by Bob Dylan

Copyright © 1962 Warner Brothers Inc.; renewed 1990 Special Rider Music.
All Rights Reserved. International Copyright Secured.

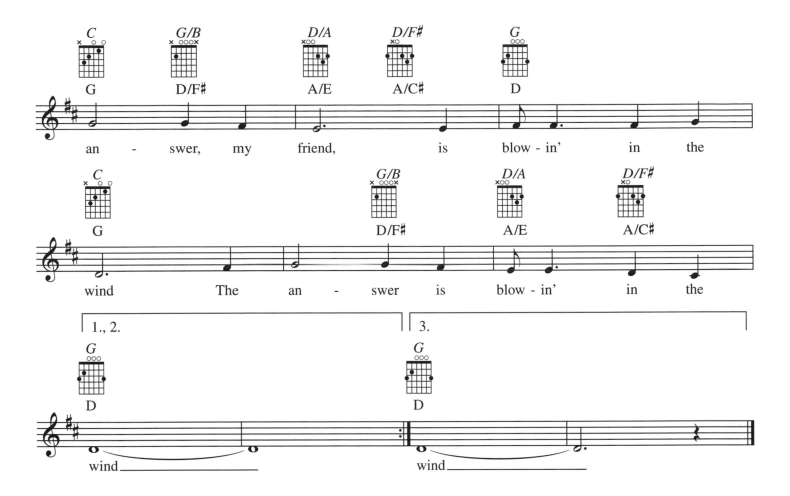

an - swer, my friend, is blow - in' in the

wind   The an - swer is blow - in' in the

1., 2.

3.

wind_____

wind_____

Additional lyrics

2. How many years can a mountain exist
   Before it's washed to the sea?
   Yes, 'n' how many years can some people exist
   Before they're allowed to be free?
   Yes, 'n' how many times can a man turn his head
   Pretending he just doesn't see?
   The answer, my friend, is blowin' in the wind
   The answer is blowin' in the wind

3. How many times must a man look up
   Before he can see the sky?
   Yes, 'n' how many ears must one man have
   Before he can hear people cry?
   Yes, 'n' how many deaths will it take till he knows
   That too many people have died?
   The answer, my friend, is blowin' in the wind
   The answer is blowin' in the wind

Long Ago, Far Away

Words and Music by Bob Dylan

Moderate hard rock

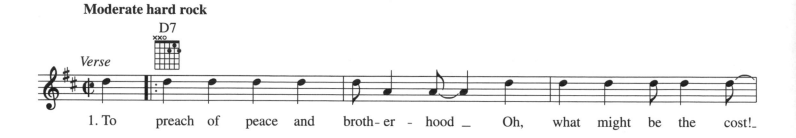

Verse

D7

1. To preach of peace and broth-er-hood __ Oh, what might be the cost!__

__ A man he did it long a-go __ And they

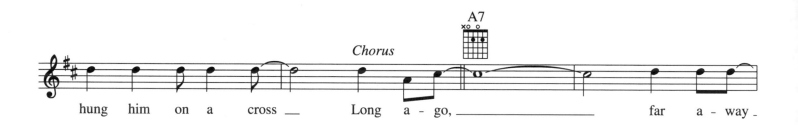

A7

Chorus

hung him on a cross __ Long a-go, _____ far a-way __

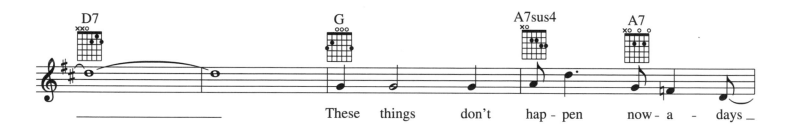

D7   G   A7sus4   A7

_____ These things don't hap-pen now-a-days __

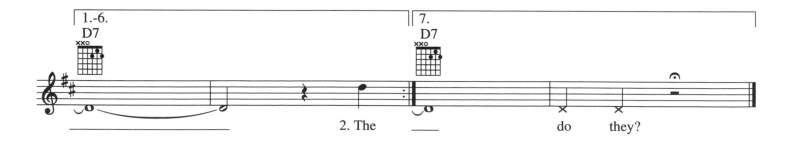

1.-6.

D7

_____

7.

D7

2. The __ do they?

Copyright © 1962, 1968 Warner Brothers Inc.; renewed 1990, 1996 Special Rider Music.
All Rights Reserved. International Copyright Secured.

Additional lyrics

2. The chains of slaves
   They dragged the ground
   With heads and hearts hung low
   But it was during Lincoln's time
   And it was long ago
   Long ago, far away
   Things like that don't happen
   No more, nowadays

3. The war guns they went off wild
   The whole world bled its blood
   Men's bodies floated on the edge
   Of oceans made of mud
   Long ago, far away
   Those kind of things don't happen
   No more, nowadays

4. One man had much money
   One man had not enough to eat
   One man lived just like a king
   The other man begged on the street
   Long ago, far away
   These things don't happen
   No more, nowadays

5. One man died of a knife so sharp
   One man died from the bullet of a gun
   One man died of a broken heart
   To see the lynchin' of his son
   Long ago, far away
   Things like that don't happen
   No more, nowadays

6. Gladiators killed themselves
   It was during the Roman times
   People cheered with bloodshot grins
   As eye and minds went blind
   Long ago, far away
   Things like that don't happen
   No more, nowadays

7. And to talk of peace and brotherhood
   Oh, what might be the cost!
   A man he did it long ago
   And they hung him on a cross
   Long ago, far away
   Things like that don't happen
   No more, nowadays, do they?

A Hard Rain's A-Gonna Fall

Words and Music by Bob Dylan

Copyright © 1963 Warner Brothers Inc.; renewed 1991 Special Rider Music.
All Rights Reserved. International Copyright Secured.

Additional lyrics

2. Oh, what did you see, my blue-eyed son?
   Oh, what did you see, my darling young one?

   I saw a newborn baby with wild wolves all around it
   I saw a highway of diamonds with nobody on it
   I saw a black branch with blood that kept drippin'
   I saw a room full of men with their hammers a-bleedin'
   I saw a white ladder all covered with water
   I saw ten thousand talkers whose tongues were all broken
   I saw guns and sharp swords in the hands of young children
   And it's a hard, and it's a hard, it's a hard, it's a hard
   And it's a hard rain's a-gonna fall

3. And what did you hear, my blue-eyed son?
   And what did you hear, my darling young one?

   I heard the sound of a thunder, it roared out a warnin'
   Heard the roar of a wave that could drown the whole world
   Heard one hundred drummers whose hands were a-blazin'
   Heard ten thousand whisperin' and nobody listenin'
   Heard one person starve, I heard many people laughin'
   Heard the song of a poet who died in the gutter
   Heard the sound of a clown who cried in the alley
   And it's a hard, and it's a hard, it's a hard, it's a hard
   And it's a hard rain's a-gonna fall

4. Oh, who did you meet, my blue-eyed son?
   Who did you meet, my darling young one?

   I met a young child beside a dead pony
   I met a white man who walked a black dog
   I met a young woman whose body was burning
   I met a young girl, she gave me a rainbow
   I met one man who was wounded in love
   I met another man who was wounded with hatred
   And it's a hard, it's a hard, it's a hard, it's a hard
   It's a hard rain's a-gonna fall

5. Oh, what'll you do now, my blue-eyed son?
   Oh, what'll you do now, my darling young one?

   I'm a-goin' back out 'fore the rain starts a-fallin'
   I'll walk to the depths of the deepest black forest
   Where the people are many and their hands are all empty
   Where the pellets of poison are flooding their waters
   Where the home in the valley meets the damp dirty prison
   Where the executioner's face is always well hidden
   Where hunger is ugly, where souls are forgotten
   Where black is the color, where none is the number
   And I'll tell it and think it and speak it and breathe it
   And reflect it from the mountain so all souls can see it
   Then I'll stand on the ocean until I start sinkin'
   But I'll know my song well before I start singin'
   And it's a hard, it's a hard, it's a hard, it's a hard
   It's a hard rain's a-gonna fall

The Death Of Emmett Till

Words and Music by Bob Dylan

Copyright © 1963, 1968 Warner Brothers Inc.; renewed 1991, 1996 Special Rider Music.
All Rights Reserved. International Copyright Secured.

Additional lyrics

2. Some men they dragged him to a barn and there they beat him up
   They said they had a reason, but I can't remember what
   They tortured him and did some things too evil to repeat
   There were screaming sounds inside the barn, there was laughing sounds out on the street

3. Then they rolled his body down a gulf amidst a bloody red rain
   And they threw him in the waters wide to cease his screaming pain
   The reason that they killed him there, and I'm sure it ain't no lie
   Was just for the fun of killin' him and to watch him slowly die

4. And then to stop the United States of yelling for a trial
   Two brothers they confessed that they had killed poor Emmett Till
   But on the jury there were men who helped the brothers commit this awful crime
   And so this trial was a mockery, but nobody seemed to mind

5. I saw the morning papers but I could not bear to see
   The smiling brothers walkin' down the courthouse stairs
   For the jury found them innocent and the brothers they went free
   While Emmett's body floats the foam of a Jim Crow southern sea

6. If you can't speak out against this kind of thing, a crime that's so unjust
   Your eyes are filled with dead men's dirt, your mind is filled with dust
   Your arms and legs they must be in shackles and chains, and your blood it must refuse to flow
   For you let this human race fall down so God-awful low!

7. This song is just a reminder to remind your fellow man
   That this kind of thing still lives today in that ghost-robed Ku Klux Klan
   But if all of us folks that thinks alike, if we gave all we could give
   We could make this great land of ours a greater place to live

Let Me Die In My Footsteps

Words and Music by Bob Dylan

Copyright © 1963, 1965 Warner Brothers Inc.; renewed 1991, 1993 Special Rider Music.
All Rights Reserved. International Copyright Secured.

Additional lyrics

3. I don't know if I'm smart but I think I can see
   When someone is pullin' the wool over me
   And if this war comes and death's all around
   Let me die on this land 'fore I die underground
   Let me die in my footsteps
   Before I go down under the ground

4. There's always been people that have to cause fear
   They've been talking of the war now for many long years
   I have read all their statements and I've not said a word
   But now Lawd God, let my poor voice be heard
   Let me die in my footsteps
   Before I go down under the ground

5. If I had rubies and riches and crowns
   I'd buy the whole world and change things around
   I'd throw all the guns and the tanks in the sea
   For they are mistakes of a past history
   Let me die in my footsteps
   Before I go down under the ground

6. Let me drink from the waters where the mountain streams flood
   Let me smell of wildflowers flow free through my blood
   Let me sleep in your meadows with the green grassy leaves
   Let me walk down the highway with my brother in peace
   Let me die in my footsteps
   Before I go down under the ground

7. Go out in your country where the land meets the sun
   See the craters and the canyons where the waterfalls run
   Nevada, New Mexico, Arizona, Idaho
   Let every state in this union seep in your souls
   And you'll die in your footsteps
   Before you go down under the ground

Ballad Of Hollis Brown

Words and Music by Bob Dylan

Copyright © 1963 Warner Brothers Inc.; renewed 1991 Special Rider Music.
All Rights Reserved. International Copyright Secured.

Additional lyrics

2. Your baby's eyes look crazy
   They're a-tuggin' at your sleeve
   Your baby's eyes look crazy
   They're a-tuggin' at your sleeve
   You walk the floor and wonder why
   With every breath you breathe

3. The rats have got your flour
   Bad blood it got your mare
   The rats have got your flour
   Bad blood it got your mare
   If there's anyone that knows
   Is there anyone that cares?

4. You prayed to the Lord above
   Oh please send you a friend
   You prayed to the Lord above
   Oh please send you a friend
   Your empty pockets tell yuh
   That you ain't a-got no friend

5. Your babies are crying louder
   It's pounding on your brain
   Your babies are crying louder now
   It's pounding on your brain
   Your wife's screams are stabbin' you
   Like the dirty drivin' rain

6. Your grass it is turning black
   There's no water in your well
   Your grass is turning black
   There's no water in your well
   You spent your last lone dollar
   On seven shotgun shells

7. Way out in the wilderness
   A cold coyote calls
   Way out in the wilderness
   A cold coyote calls
   Your eyes fix on the shotgun
   That's hangin' on the wall

8. Your brain is a-bleedin'
   And your legs can't seem to stand
   Your brain is a-bleedin'
   And your legs can't seem to stand
   Your eyes fix on the shotgun
   That you're holdin' in your hand

9. There's seven breezes a-blowin'
   All around the cabin door
   There's seven breezes a-blowin'
   All around the cabin door
   Seven shots ring out
   Like the ocean's pounding roar

10. There's seven people dead
    On a South Dakota farm
    There's seven people dead
    On a South Dakota farm
    Somewhere in the distance
    There's seven new people born

Quit Your Low Down Ways

Words and Music by Bob Dylan

Copyright © 1963, 1964 Warner Brothers Inc.; renewed 1991, 1992 Special Rider Music.
All Rights Reserved. International Copyright Secured.

Additional lyrics

2. Well, you can run down to the White House
   You can gaze at the Capitol Dome, pretty mama
   You can pound on the President's gate
   But you oughta know by now it's gonna be too late

Refrain

3. Well, you can run down to the desert
   Throw yourself on the burning sand
   You can raise up your right hand, pretty mama
   But you better understand you done lost your one good man

Refrain

4. And you can hitchhike on the highway
   You can stand all alone by the side of the road
   You can try to flag a ride back home, pretty mama
   But you can't ride in my car no more

Refrain

5. Oh, you can read out your Bible
   You can fall down on your knees, pretty mama
   And pray to the Lord
   But it ain't gonna do no good

Refrain

Baby, I'm In The Mood For You

Words and Music by Bob Dylan

Copyright © 1963, 1966 Warner Brothers Inc.; renewed 1991, 1994 Special Rider Music.
All Rights Reserved. International Copyright Secured.

Additional lyrics

2. Sometimes I'm in the mood, Lord, I had my overflowin' fill
   Sometimes I'm in the mood, I'm gonna make out my final will
   Sometimes I'm in the mood, I'm gonna head for the walkin' hill
   But then again, but then again, I said oh, I said oh, I said
   Oh babe, I'm in the mood for you

3. Sometimes I'm in the mood, I wanna lay right down and die
   Sometimes I'm in the mood, I wanna climb up to the sky
   Sometimes I'm in the mood, I'm gonna laugh until I cry
   But then again, I said again, I said again, I said
   Oh babe, I'm in the mood for you

4. Sometimes I'm in the mood, I'm gonna sleep in my pony's stall
   Sometimes I'm in the mood, I ain't gonna do nothin' at all
   Sometimes I'm in the mood, I wanna fly like a cannon ball
   But then again, but then again, I said oh, I said oh, I said
   Oh babe, I'm in the mood for you

5. Sometimes I'm in the mood, I wanna back up against the wall
   Sometimes I'm in the mood, I wanna run till I have to crawl
   Sometimes I'm in the mood, I ain't gonna do nothin' at all
   But then again, but then again, I said oh, I said oh, I said
   Oh babe, I'm in the mood for you

6. Sometimes I'm in the mood, I wanna change my house around
   Sometimes I'm in the mood, I'm gonna make a change in this here town
   Sometimes I'm in the mood, I'm gonna change the world around
   But then again, but then again, I said oh, I said oh, I said
   Oh babe, I'm in the mood for you

All Over You

Words and Music by Bob Dylan

Copyright © 1968 Warner Bros. Inc.; renewed 1996 Special Rider Music.
All Rights Reserved. International Copyright Secured.

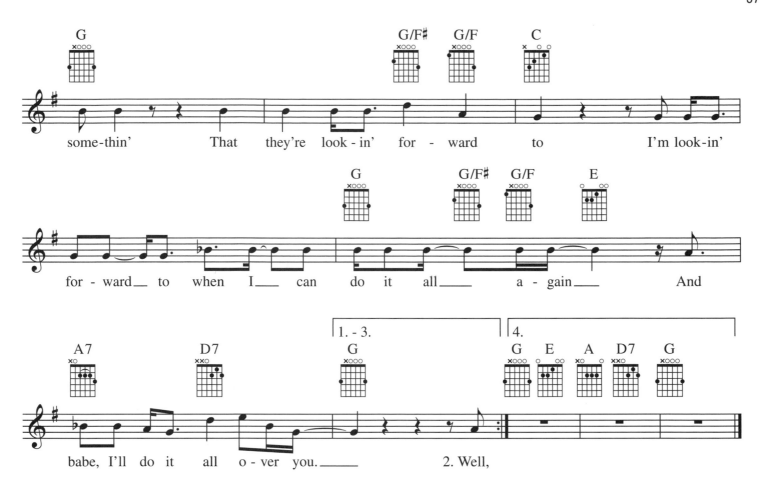

some-thin' That they're look - in' for - ward to I'm look - in'

for - ward__ to when I__ can do it all____ a - gain____ And

babe, I'll do it all o - ver you. ____ 2. Well,

Additional lyrics

2. Well, if I had my way tomorrow or today
   Babe, I'd run circles all around
   I'd jump up in the wind, do a somersault and spin
   I'd even dance a jig on the ground
   Well, everybody gets their hour
   Everybody gets their time
   Little David when he picked up his pebbles
   Even Sampson after he went blind
   Well, everybody gets the chance
   To do what they want to do
   When my time arrives you better run for your life
   'Cause babe, I'll do it all over you

3. Well, I don't need no money, I just need a day that's sunny
   Baby, and my days are gonna come
   And I grab me a pint, you know that I'm a giant
   When you hear me yellin', "Fee-fi-fo-fum"
   Well, you cut me like a jigsaw puzzle
   You made me to a walkin' wreck
   Then you pushed my heart through my backbone
   Then you knocked off my head from my neck
   Well, if I'm ever standin' steady
   A-doin' what I want to do
   Well, I tell you little lover that you better run for cover
   'Cause babe, I'll do it all over you

4. I'm just restin' at your gate so that I won't be late
   And, momma, I'm a-just sittin' on the shelf
   Look out your window fair and you'll see me squattin' there
   Just a-fumblin' and a-mumblin' to myself
   Well, after my cigarette's been smoked up
   After all my liquor's been drunk
   After my dreams are dreamed out
   After all my thoughts have been thunk
   Well, after I do some of these things
   I'm gonna do what I have to do
   And I tell you on the side, that you better run and hide
   'Cause babe, I'll do it all over you

I'd Hate To Be You On That Dreadful Day

Words and Music by Bob Dylan

Moderate boogie-rock

1. Well, your clock is gon-na stop At Saint Pe-ter's gate __ Ya gon-na
4. have to walk __ na-ked Can't ride in no car __ You're gon-na

ask him what time it is He's gon-na say, "It's too late" __ Hey, hey! I'd
let ev-'ry-bod-y see _____ Just what you __ are __

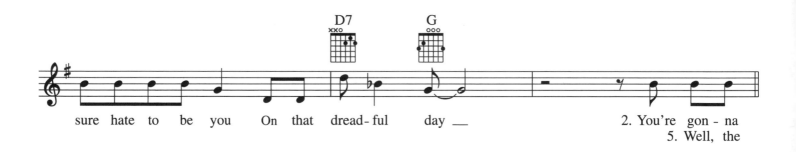

sure hate to be you On that dread-ful day __ 2. You're gon-na
5. Well, the

start to sweat __ And you ain't gon-na stop __ You're gon-na have a night-mare And
good wine's a-flow-in' For five cents a quart __ You're gon-na look in your mon-ey-bags And

Copyright © 1964, 1967 Warner Brothers Inc.; renewed 1992, 1995 Special Rider Music.
All Rights Reserved. International Copyright Secured.

Long Time Gone

Words and Music by Bob Dylan

Copyright © 1963, 1968 Warner Brothers Inc.; renewed 1991, 1996 Special Rider Music.
All Rights Reserved. International Copyright Secured.

Additional lyrics

2. On the western side of Texas
   On the Texas plains
   I tried to find a job o'work
   But they said I's young of age
   My eyes they burned when I heard
   "Go home where you belong!"
   I'm a long time a-comin'
   An' I'll be a long time gone

3. I remember when I's ramblin'
   Around with the carnival trains
   Different towns, different people
   Somehow they're all the same
   I remember children's faces best
   I remember travelin' on
   I'm a long time a-comin'
   I'll be a long time gone

4. I once loved a fair young maid
   An' I ain't too big to tell
   If she broke my heart a single time
   She broke it ten or twelve
   I walked and talked all by myself
   I did not tell no one
   I'm a long time a-comin', babe
   An' I'll be a long time gone

5. Many times by the highwayside
   I tried to flag a ride
   With bloodshot eyes and gritting teeth
   I'd watch the cars roll by
   The empty air hung in my head
   I's thinkin' all day long
   I'm a long time a-comin'
   I'll be a long time gone

6. You might see me on your crossroads
   When I'm a-passin' through
   Remember me how you wished to
   As I'm a-driftin' from your view
   I ain't got the time to think about it
   I got too much to get done
   Well, I'm a long time comin'
   An' I'll be a long time gone

7. If I can't help somebody
   With a word or song
   If I can't show somebody
   They are travelin' wrong
   But I know I ain't no prophet
   An' I ain't no prophet's son
   I'm just a long time a-comin'
   An' I'll be a long time gone

8. So you can have your beauty
   It's skin deep and it only lies
   And you can have your youth
   It'll rot before your eyes
   Just give to me my gravestone
   With it clearly carved upon:
   "I's a long time a-comin'
   An' I'll be a long time gone "

Talkin' John Birch Paranoid Blues

Words and Music by Bob Dylan

Copyright © 1970 Special Rider Music.
All Rights Reserved. International Copyright Secured.

Additional lyrics

2. So I run down most hurriedly
   And joined up with the John Birch Society
   I got me a secret membership card
   And started off a-walkin' down the road
   Yee-hoo, I'm a real John Bircher now!
   Look out you Commies!

3. Now we all agree with Hitler's views
   Although he killed six million Jews
   It don't matter too much that he was a Fascist
   At least you can't say he was a Communist!
   That's to say like if you got a cold you take a shot of malaria

4. Well, I wus lookin' everywhere for them gol-darned Reds
   I got up in the mornin' 'n' looked under my bed
   Looked in the sink, behind the door
   Looked in the glove compartment of my car
   Couldn't find 'em…

5. I wus lookin' high an' low for them Reds everywhere
   I wus lookin' in the sink an' underneath the chair
   I looked way up my chimney hole
   I even looked deep down inside my toilet bowl
   They got away…

6. Well, I wus sittin' home alone an' started to sweat
   Figured they wus in my T.V. set
   Peeked behind the picture frame
   Got a shock from my feet, hittin' right up in the brain
   Them Reds caused it!
   I know they did…them hard-core ones

7. Well, I quit my job so I could work all alone
   Then I changed my name to Sherlock Holmes
   Followed some clues from my detective bag
   And discovered they wus red stripes on the American flag!
   That ol' Betsy Ross…

8. Well, I investigated all the books in the library
   Ninety percent of 'em gotta be burned away
   I investigated all the people that I knowed
   Ninety-eight percent of them gotta go
   The other two percent are fellow Birchers…just like me

9. Now Eisenhower, he's a Russian spy
   Lincoln, Jefferson and that Roosevelt guy
   To my knowledge there's just one man
   That's really a true American: George Lincoln Rockwell
   I know for a fact he hates Commies cus he picketed the movie *Exodus*

10. Well, I fin'ly started thinkin' straight
    When I run outa things to investigate
    Couldn't imagine doin' anything else
    So now I'm sittin' home investigatin' myself!
    Hope I don't find out anything…hmm, great God!

Masters Of War

Words and Music by Bob Dylan

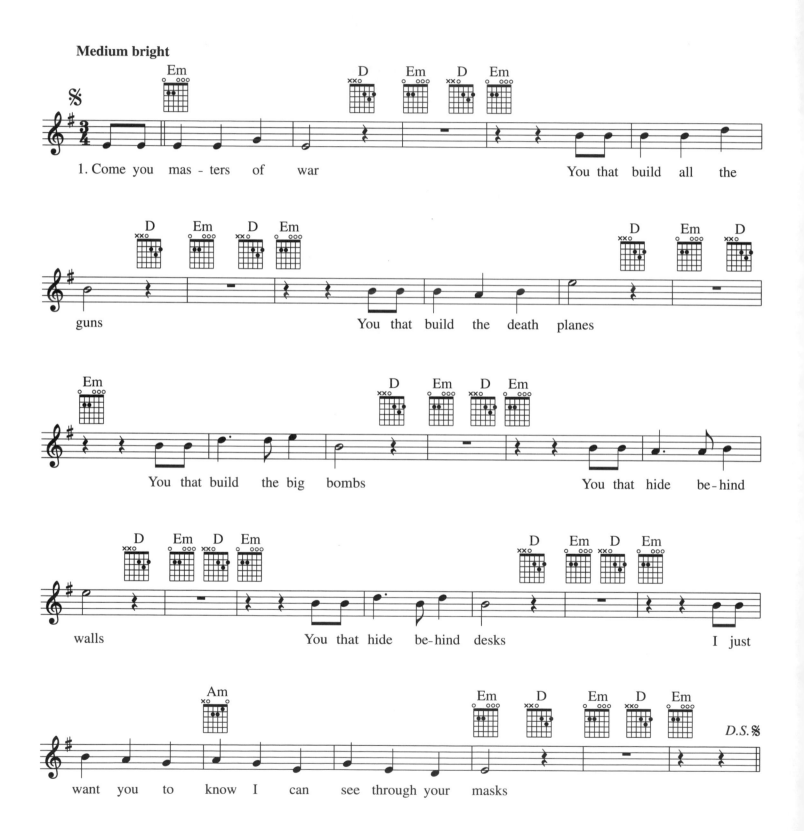

Copyright © 1963 Warner Brothers Inc.; renewed 1991 Special Rider Music.
All Rights Reserved. International Copyright Secured.

Additional lyrics

2. You that never done nothin'
   But build to destroy
   You play with my world
   Like it's your little toy
   You put a gun in my hand
   And you hide from my eyes
   And you turn and run farther
   When the fast bullets fly

3. Like Judas of old
   You lie and deceive
   A world war can be won
   You want me to believe
   But I see through your eyes
   And I see through your brain
   Like I see through the water
   That runs down my drain

4. You fasten the triggers
   For the others to fire
   Then you set back and watch
   When the death count gets higher
   You hide in your mansion
   As young people's blood
   Flows out of their bodies
   And is buried in the mud

5. You've thrown the worst fear
   That can ever be hurled
   Fear to bring children
   Into the world
   For threatening my baby
   Unborn and unnamed
   You ain't worth the blood
   That runs in your veins

6. How much do I know
   To talk out of turn
   You might say that I'm young
   You might say I'm unlearned
   But there's one thing I know
   Though I'm younger than you
   Even Jesus would never
   Forgive what you do

7. Let me ask you one question
   Is your money that good
   Will it buy you forgiveness
   Do you think that it could
   I think you will find
   When your death takes its toll
   All the money you made
   Will never buy back your soul

8. And I hope that you die
   And your death'll come soon
   I will follow your casket
   In the pale afternoon
   And I'll watch while you're lowered
   Down to your deathbed
   And I'll stand o'er your grave
   'Til I'm sure that you're dead

Oxford Town

Words and Music by Bob Dylan

Copyright © 1963 Warner Brothers Inc.; renewed 1992 Special Rider Music.
All Rights Reserved. International Copyright Secured.

Farewell

Words and Music by Bob Dylan

Copyright © 1963, 1973 Warner Brothers Inc.; renewed 1991 Special Rider Music.
All Rights Reserved. International Copyright Secured.

Additional lyrics

2. Oh the weather is against me and the wind blows hard
   And the rain she's a-turnin' into hail
   I still might strike it lucky on a highway goin' west
   Though I'm travelin' on a path beaten trail

   Refrain

3. I will write you a letter from time to time
   As I'm ramblin' you can travel with me too
   With my head, my heart and my hands, my love
   I will send what I learn back home to you

   Refrain

4. I will tell you of the laughter and of troubles
   Be them somebody else's or my own
   With my hands in my pockets and my coat collar high
   I will travel unnoticed and unknown

   Refrain

5. I've heard tell of a town where I might as well be bound
   It's down around the old Mexican plains
   They say that the people are all friendly there
   And all they ask of you is your name

   Refrain

Bound To Lose, Bound To Win

Words and Music by Bob Dylan

Copyright © 2010 Special Rider Music.
All Rights Reserved. International Copyright Secured.

IT'S ALL RIGHT

1. There ain't no use to sit and wonder why babe
Dont matter anyhow
There aint no use to sit and wonder why babe
If you don't know by now
When the rooster crows at the break of dawn
Look out your window and Ill be gone
Honey, oh the reason Im travelin on
Dont think twice, it's all right

2. Well there aint no use in turnin' on your light babe
The light i never knowed
Ther aint no use in turnin' on your light babe
I'm on the dark side ofthe road
Still i wish there was something you would do or say
To try and make me change my mind and stay
We never did too much talking anyway
So dont think twice-Its all right

3. Well there ain't no use in calling out my name babe
Like you never done before
There ain't no use in calling out my name babe
I cant hear you anymore
IM a thinkin an a wonderin all the way down the road
I once loved a woman, a child Im told
I gave her my heart but she wanted my soul
Dont think twice-Its all right

4. I'mgoing down that long lonesome road, gal
Where I'm bound for i cant tell
Goodbye's too good a word, gal
So Ill just say fare the well
NOw I aint sayin you treated me unkind
You could a done better but I don't mind
You just kind a wasted my precious time
Dont think twice-Its allright (2) Times

© 1963 BOB DYLAN

Don't Think Twice, It's All Right

Words and Music by Bob Dylan

Copyright © 1963 Warner Brothers Inc.; renewed 1991 Special Rider Music.
All Rights Reserved. International Copyright Secured.

right

3. It ain't no use ___ in call-in' out my name, gal ___
(4. I'm) walk-in' down ___ that long, lone-some road, babe ___

Like you nev-er did be-fore   It ain't no use ___ in call-in' out my
Where I'm bound, I can't ___ tell   But good-bye's   too   good a

name, gal ___   I can't hear you an-y more   I'm a-
word, gal ___   So I'll just say fare thee well   I ain't

think-in' and a-won-d'rin' all the way down the road   I once loved a wom-an,_____
say-in'   you treat-ed me un-kind   You could have done bet-ter _____

____ a child I'm told   I give her my heart but she want-ed my soul
____ but I don't mind   You just kind-a wast-ed   my pre-cious time

But don't think twice, It's all right   4. I'm right
But don't think twice, It's all

Walkin' Down The Line

Words and Music by Bob Dylan

Moderato

Refrain

Well, I'm walk - in' down the line ____ I'm walk - in' down the

line ____ An' I'm walk - in' down the line My

feet - 'll be a - flyin' To tell a - bout my trou - bled mind ____ My

fifth time Fine

1. I got a heav - y - head - ed gal ____ I got a heav - y - head - ed

gal ____ I got a heav - y - head - ed gal She

ain't ____ feel - in' well When she's bet - ter on - ly time will tell ____

to Refrain

Copyright © 1963, 1965 Warner Brothers Inc.; renewed 1991, 1993 Special Rider Music.
All Rights Reserved. International Copyright Secured.

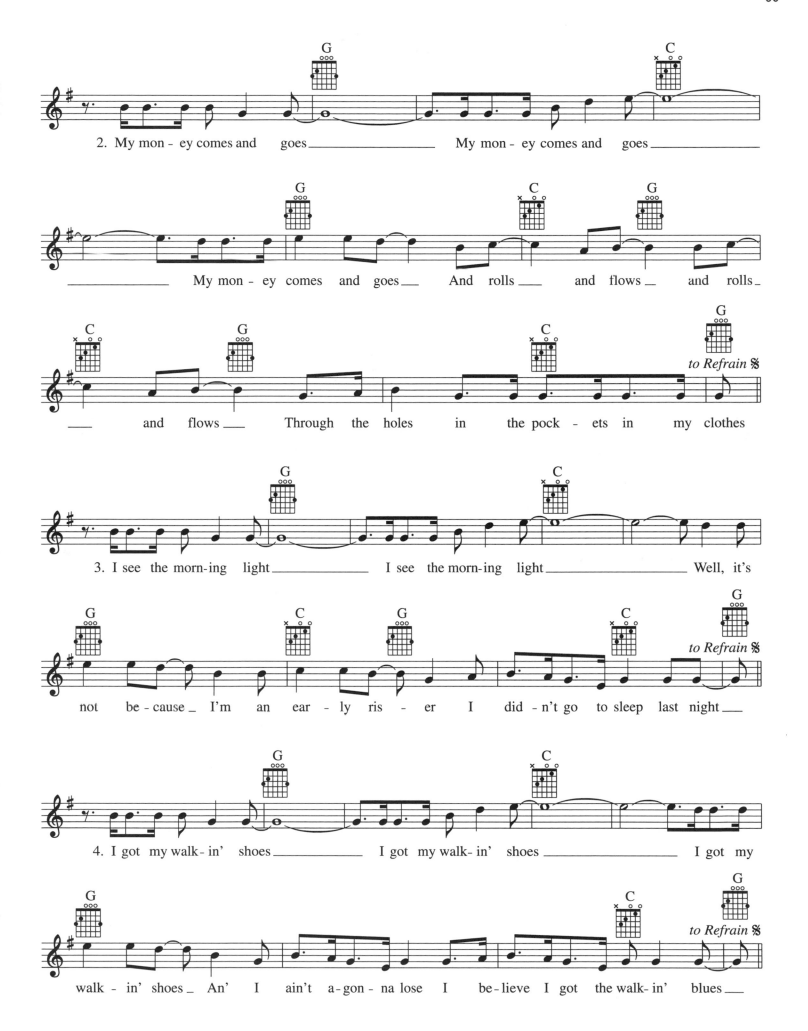

I Shall Be Free

Words and Music by Bob Dylan

Moderate country boogie

1. Well, I took me a wom-an late last night __ I's three-fourths drunk, she looked up-tight __ She took off her wheel, took off her bell Took off her wig, said, "How do I smell?" I hot-footed it... bare-na-ked... out the win-dow! 2. Well,

Additional lyrics

2. Well, sometimes I might get drunk
   Walk like a duck and stomp like a skunk
   Don't hurt me none, don't hurt my pride
   'Cause I got my little lady right by my side
   (Right there
   Proud as can be)

3. I's out there paintin' on the old woodshed
   When a can a black paint it fell on my head
   I went down to scrub and rub
   But I had to sit in back of the tub
   (Cost a quarter
   And I had to get out quick . . .
   Someone wanted to come in and take a sauna)

Copyright © 1963, 1967 Warner Brothers Inc.; renewed 1991, 1995 Special Rider Music.
All Rights Reserved. International Copyright Secured.

4. Well, my telephone rang it would not stop
It's President Kennedy callin' me up
He said, "My friend, Bob, what do we need to make the country grow?"
I said, "My friend, John, Brigitte Bardot
Anita Ekberg
Sophia Loren"
(Put 'em all in the same room with Ernest Borgnine!)

5. Well, I got a woman sleeps on a cot
She yells and hollers and squeals a lot
Licks my face and tickles my ear
Bends me over and buys me beer
(She's a honeymooner
A June crooner
A spoon feeder
And a natural leader)

6. Oh, there ain't no use in me workin' so heavy
I got a woman who works on the levee
Pumping that water up to her neck
Every week she sends me a monthly check
(She's a humdinger
Folk singer
Dead ringer
For a thing-a-muh jigger)

7. Late one day in the middle of the week
Eyes were closed I was half asleep
I chased me a woman up the hill
Right in the middle of an air-raid drill
It was Little Bo Peep!
(I jumped a fallout shelter
I jumped a bean stalk
I jumped a Ferris wheel)

8. Now, the man on the stand he wants my vote
He's a-runnin' for office on the ballot note
He's out there preachin' in front of the steeple
Tellin' me he loves all kinds-a people
(He's eatin' bagels
He's eatin' pizza
He's eatin' chitlins
He's eatin' bullshit!)

9. Oh, set me down on a television floor
I'll flip the channel to number four
Out of the shower comes a grown-up man
With a bottle of hair oil in his hand
(It's that greasy kid stuff
What I want to know, Mr. Football Man, is
What do you do about Willy Mays and Yul Brynner
Charles de Gaulle
And Robert Louis Stevenson?)

10. Well, the funniest woman I ever seen
Was the great-granddaughter of Mr. Clean
She takes about fifteen baths a day
Wants me to grow a cigar on my face
(She's a little bit heavy!)

11. Well, ask me why I'm drunk alla time
It levels my head and eases my mind
I just walk along and stroll and sing
I see better days and I do better things
(I catch dinosaurs
I make love to Elizabeth Taylor . . .
Catch hell from Richard Burton!)

Bob Dylan's Blues

Words and Music by Bob Dylan

Well, the Lone Rang - er and Ton - to They are rid - in' down the line __

__ Fix - in' ev - 'ry - bod - y's trou - bles _____ Ev - 'ry - bod - y's 'cept

repeat four times

mine Some - bod - y must - a tol' 'em That I was do - in' fine __

Additional lyrics

2. Oh you five and ten cent women
   With nothin' in your heads
   I got a real gal I'm lovin'
   And Lord I'll love her till I'm dead
   Go away from my door and my window too
   Right now

3. Lord, I ain't goin' down to no race track
   See no sports car run
   I don't have no sports car
   And I don't even care to have one
   I can walk anytime around the block

4. Well, the wind keeps a-blowin' me
   Up and down the street
   With my hat in my hand
   And my boots on my feet
   Watch out so you don't step on me

5. Well, lookit here buddy
   You want to be like me
   Pull out your six-shooter
   And rob every bank you can see
   Tell the judge I said it was all right
   Yes!

Copyright © 1963, 1966 Warner Brothers Inc.; renewed 1991, 1994 Special Rider Music.
All Rights Reserved. International Copyright Secured.

Girl From The North Country

Words and Music by Bob Dylan

Moderato, gently

1. Well, if you're trav - 'lin' in the north coun - try fair

Where the winds hit heav - y on the bor - der - line _____ Re -

mem - ber me to one who lives there

She once was _____ a true love of mine

Additional lyrics

2. Well, if you go when the snowflakes storm
   When the rivers freeze and summer ends
   Please see if she's wearing a coat so warm
   To keep her from the howlin' winds

3. Please see for me if her hair hangs long
   If it rolls and flows all down her breast
   Please see for me if her hair hangs long
   That's the way I remember her best

4. I'm a-wonderin' if she remembers me at all
   Many times I've often prayed
   In the darkness of my night
   In the brightness of my day

5. So if you're travelin' in the north country fair
   Where the winds hit heavy on the borderline
   Remember me to one who lives there
   She once was a true love of mine

Copyright © 1963 Warner Brothers Inc.; renewed 1991Special Rider Music.
All Rights Reserved. International Copyright Secured.

Bob Dylan's Dream

Words and Music by Bob Dylan

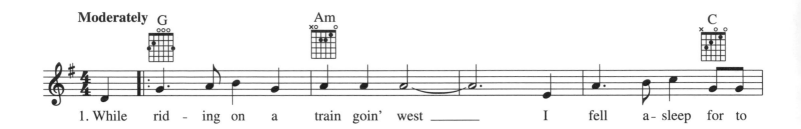

1. While rid - ing on a train goin' west _____ I fell a- sleep for to

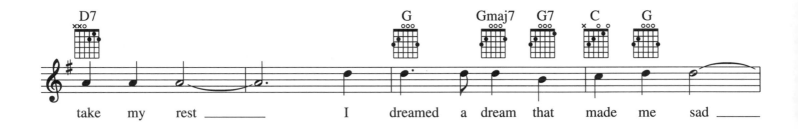

take my rest _____ I dreamed a dream that made me sad _____

____ Con - cern - ing my- self _____ And the first few friends I

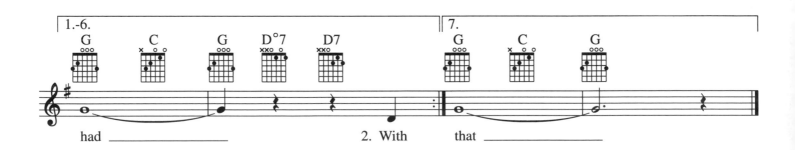

had _____ 2. With that _____

Copyright © 1963, 1964 Warner Brothers Inc.; renewed 1991, 1992 Special Rider Music.
All Rights Reserved. International Copyright Secured.

Additional lyrics

2. With half-damp eyes I stared to the room
   Where my friends and I spent many an afternoon
   Where we together weathered many a storm
   Laughin' and singin' till the early hours of the morn

3. By the old wooden stove where our hats was hung
   Our words were told, our songs were sung
   Where we longed for nothin' and were quite satisfied
   Talkin' and a-jokin' about the world outside

4. With haunted hearts through the heat and cold
   We never thought we could ever get old
   We thought we could sit forever in fun
   But our chances really was a million to one

5. As easy it was to tell black from white
   It was all that easy to tell wrong from right
   And our choices were few and the thought never hit
   That the one road we traveled would ever shatter and split

6. How many a year has passed and gone
   And many a gamble has been lost and won
   And many a road taken by many a friend
   And each one I've never seen again

7. I wish, I wish, I wish in vain
   That we could sit simply in that room again
   Ten thousand dollars at the drop of a hat
   I'd give it all gladly if our lives could be like that

Boots Of Spanish Leather

Words and Music by Bob Dylan

Slowly
Refrain

1. Oh, I'm sail - in' a - way my ___ own true

love I'm sail - in' a - way in the morn - ing ___

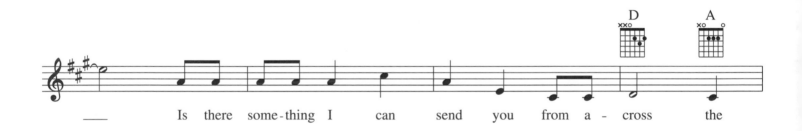

___ Is there some - thing I can send you from a - cross the

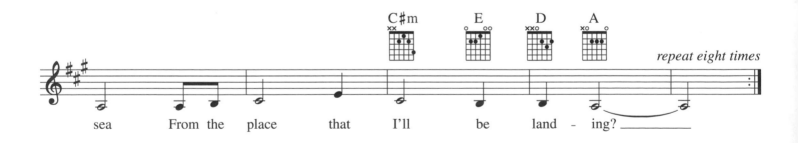

repeat eight times

sea From the place that I'll be land - ing? ___

Copyright © 1963, 1964 Warner Brothers Inc.; renewed 1991, 1992 Special Rider Music, USA.
All Rights Reserved. International Copyright Secured.

Additional lyrics

2. No, there's nothin' you can send me, my own true love
   There's nothin' I wish to be ownin'
   Just carry yourself back to me unspoiled
   From across that lonesome ocean

3. Oh, but I just thought you might want something fine
   Made of silver or of golden
   Either from the mountains of Madrid
   Or from the coast of Barcelona

4. Oh, but if I had the stars from the darkest night
   And the diamonds from the deepest ocean
   I'd forsake them all for your sweet kiss
   For that's all I'm wishin' to be ownin'

5. That I might be gone a long time
   And it's only that I'm askin'
   Is there something I can send you to remember me by
   To make your time more easy passin'

6. Oh, how can, how can you ask me again
   It only brings me sorrow
   The same thing I want from you today
   I would want again tomorrow

7. I got a letter on a lonesome day
   It was from her ship a-sailin'
   Saying I don't know when I'll be comin' back again
   It depends on how I'm a-feelin'

8. Well, if you, my love, must think that-a-way
   I'm sure your mind is roamin'
   I'm sure your heart is not with me
   But with the country to where you're goin'

9. So take heed, take heed of the western wind
   Take heed of the stormy weather
   And yes, there's something you can send back to me
   Spanish boots of Spanish leather

Seven Curses

Words and Music by Bob Dylan

Slowly and sadly

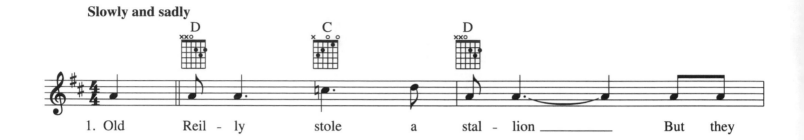

1. Old Reil - ly stole a stal - lion _____ But they

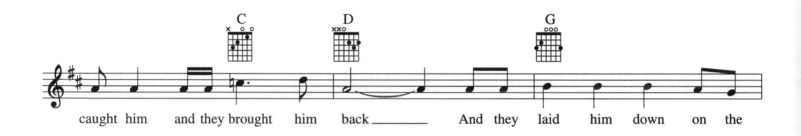

caught him and they brought him back _____ And they laid him down on the

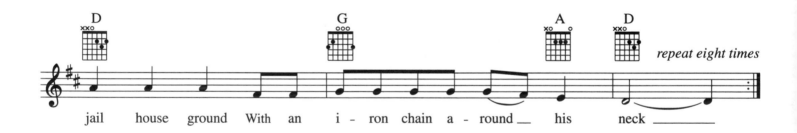

repeat eight times

jail house ground With an i - ron chain a - round _ his neck _____

Copyright © 1963, 1974 Warner Brothers Inc.; renewed 1991 Special Rider Music.
All Rights Reserved. International Copyright Secured.

Additional lyrics

2. Old Reilly's daughter got a message
   That her father was goin' to hang
   She rode by night and came by morning
   With gold and silver in her hand

3. When the judge he saw Reilly's daughter
   His old eyes deepened in his head
   Sayin', "Gold will never free your father
   The price, my dear, is you instead"

4. "Oh I'm as good as dead," cried Reilly
   "It's only you that he does crave
   And my skin will surely crawl if he touches you at all
   Get on your horse and ride away"

5. "Oh father you will surely die
   If I don't take the chance to try
   And pay the price and not take your advice
   For that reason I will have to stay"

6. The gallows shadows shook the evening
   In the night a hound dog bayed
   In the night the grounds were groanin'
   In the night the price was paid

7. The next mornin' she had awoken
   To know that the judge had never spoken
   She saw that hangin' branch a-bendin'
   She saw her father's body broken

8. These be seven curses on a judge so cruel:
   That one doctor will not save him
   That two healers will not heal him
   That three eyes will not see him

9. That four ears will not hear him
   That five walls will not hide him
   That six diggers will not bury him
   And that seven deaths shall never kill him

Hero Blues

Words and Music by Bob Dylan

Copyright © 1963 Warner Brothers Inc.; renewed 1991 Special Rider Music.
All Rights Reserved. International Copyright Secured.

Whatcha Gonna Do?

Words and Music by Bob Dylan

Moderato

1. Tell me what____ you're gon - na do When the shad-ow comes un - der your door ____

____ Tell me what____ you're gon - na do When the

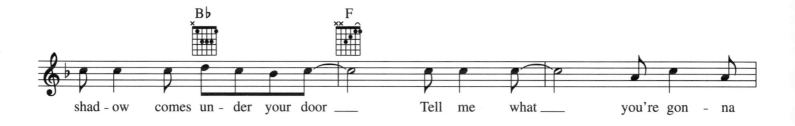

shad - ow comes un - der your door ____ Tell me what____ you're gon - na

do When the shad - ow comes un - der your door ____ O Lord, O

Lord What shall you do? ____ 2. Tell me what____

Copyright © 1963, 1966 Warner Brothers Inc.; renewed 1991, 1994 Special Rider Music.
All Rights Reserved. International Copyright Secured.

Additional lyrics

2. Tell me what you're gonna do
   When the devil calls your cards
   Tell me what you're gonna do
   When the devil calls your cards
   Tell me what you're gonna do
   When the devil calls your cards
   O Lord, O Lord
   What shall you do?

3. Tell me what you're gonna do
   When your water turns to wine
   Tell me what you're gonna do
   When your water turns to wine
   Tell me what you're gonna do
   When your water turns to wine
   O Lord, O Lord
   What should you do?

4. Tell me what you're gonna do
   When you can't play God no more
   Tell me what you're gonna do
   When you can't play God no more
   Tell me what you're gonna do
   When you can't play God no more
   O Lord, O Lord
   What shall you do?

5. Tell me what you're gonna do
   When the shadow comes creepin' in your room
   Tell me what you're gonna do
   When the shadow comes creepin' in your room
   Tell me what you're gonna do
   When the shadow comes creepin' in your room
   O Lord, O Lord
   What should you do?

Gypsy Lou

Words and Music by Bob Dylan

Copyright © 1963, 1966 Warner Brothers Inc.; renewed 1991, 1994 Special Rider Music.
All Rights Reserved. International Copyright Secured.

Additional lyrics

2. Well, I seen the whole country through
   Just to find Gypsy Lou
   Seen it up, seen it down
   Followin' Gypsy Lou around
   Hey, 'round the bend
   Gypsy Lou's gone again
   Gypsy Lou's gone again

3. Well, I gotta stop and take some rest
   My poor feet are second best
   My poor feet are wearin' thin
   Gypsy Lou's gone again
   Hey, gone again
   Gypsy Lou's 'round the bend
   Gypsy Lou's 'round the bend

4. Well, seen her up in old Cheyenne
   Turned my head and away she ran
   From Denver Town to Wichita
   Last I heard she's in Arkansas
   Hey, 'round the bend
   Gypsy Lou's gone again
   Gypsy Lou's gone again

5. Well, I tell you what if you want to do
   Tell you what, you'll wear out your shoes
   If you want to wear out your shoes
   Try and follow Gypsy Lou
   Hey, gone again
   Gypsy Lou's 'round the bend
   Gypsy Lou's 'round the bend

6. Well, Gypsy Lou, I been told
   Livin' down on Gallus Road
   Gallus Road, Arlington
   Moved away to Washington
   Hey, 'round the bend
   Gypsy Lou's gone again
   Gypsy Lou's gone again

7. Well, I went down to Washington
   Then she went to Oregon
   I skipped the ground and hopped a train
   She's back in Gallus Road again
   Hey, I can't win
   Gypsy Lou's gone again
   Gypsy Lou's gone again

8. Well, the last I heard of Gypsy Lou
   She's in a Memphis calaboose
   She left one too many a boy behind
   He committed suicide
   Hey, you can't win
   Gypsy Lou's gone again
   Gypsy Lou's gone again

Ain't Gonna Grieve

Words and Music by Bob Dylan

Moderate gospel tempo

Chorus

Well, I ain't a - gon - na grieve no more, no more

Ain't a - gon - na grieve no more, no more Ain't a - gon - na grieve no

more, no more And I ain't a - gon - na grieve no more _____ *Last time end here*

Verse

1. Come on broth - ers, join the band _ Come on sis - ters, clap your hands _

Tell ev - 'ry - bod - y that's in the land You ain't a - gon - na grieve no more Well, I

D.S. 𝄋

Copyright © 1963, 1968 Warner Brothers Inc.; renewed 1991, 1996 Special Rider Music.
All Rights Reserved. International Copyright Secured.

Additional lyrics

2. Brown and blue and white and black
   All one color on the one-way track
   We got this far and ain't a-goin' back
   And I ain't a-gonna grieve no more

   Chorus

3. We're gonna notify your next of kin
   You're gonna raise the roof until the house falls in
   If you get knocked down get up again
   We ain't a-gonna grieve no more

   Chorus

4. We'll sing this song all night long
   Sing it to my baby from midnight on
   She'll sing it to you when I'm dead and gone
   Ain't a-gonna grieve no more

   Chorus

John Brown

Words and Music by Bob Dylan

Moderate rock

1. John Brown went off to war to fight on a for - eign shore His
2. son, you look so fine, I'm glad you're a son of mine You
3. that old train pulled out, John's _ ma be - gan to shout Tell-in'
4. let - ter once in a while and her face broke in - to a smile As she

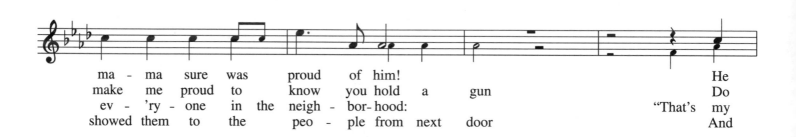

ma - ma sure was proud of him! He
make me proud to know you hold a gun Do
ev - 'ry - one in the neigh - bor - hood: "That's my
showed them to the peo - ple from next door And

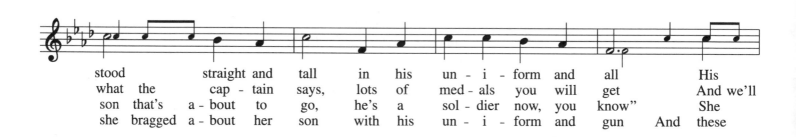

stood straight and tall in his un - i - form and all His
what the cap - tain says, lots of med - als you will get And we'll
son that's a - bout to go, he's a sol - dier now, you know" She
she bragged a - bout her son with his un - i - form and gun And these

to Coda
for final ending ⊕ | 1.2.3.

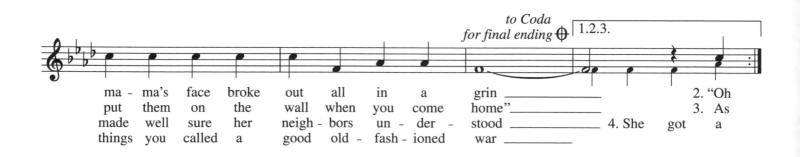

ma - ma's face broke out all in a grin _____ 2. "Oh
put them on the wall when you come home" _____ 3. As
made well sure her neigh - bors un - der - stood _____ 4. She got a
things you called a good old - fash - ioned war _____

Copyright © 1963, 1968 Warner Brothers Inc.; renewed 1991, 1996 Special Rider Music.
All Rights Reserved. International Copyright Secured.

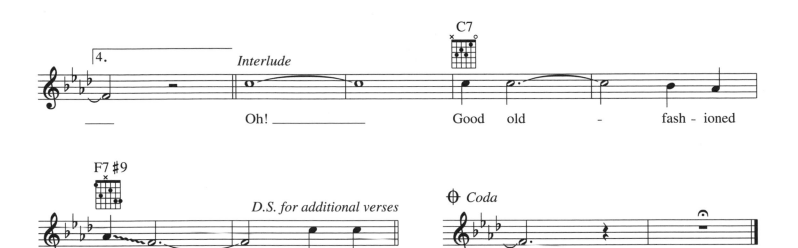

Interlude

Oh! _____ Good old - fash - ioned

D.S. for additional verses

war! _____ 5. Then the

Coda

_____

Additional lyrics

5. Then the letters ceased to come, for a long time they did not come
   They ceased to come for about ten months or more
   Then a letter finally came saying, "Go down and meet the train
   Your son's a-coming home from the war"

6. She smiled and went right down, she looked everywhere around
   But she could not see her soldier son in sight
   But as all the people passed, she saw her son at last
   When she did she could hardly believe her eyes

7. Oh his face was all shot up and his hand was all blown off
   And he wore a metal brace around his waist
   He whispered kind of slow, in a voice she did not know
   While she couldn't even recognize his face!

   Oh! Lord! Not even recognize his face

8. "Oh tell me, my darling son, pray tell me what they done
   How is it you come to be this way?"
   He tried his best to talk but his mouth could hardly move
   And the mother had to turn her face away

9. "Don't you remember, Ma, when I went off to war
   You thought it was the best thing I could do?
   I was on the battleground, you were home . . . acting proud
   You wasn't there standing in my shoes"

10. "Oh, and I thought when I was there, God, what am I doing here?
    I'm a-tryin' to kill somebody or die tryin'
    But the thing that scared me most was when my enemy came close
    And I saw that his face looked just like mine"

    Oh! Lord! Just like mine!

11. "And I couldn't help but think, through the thunder rolling and stink
    That I was just a puppet in a play
    And through the roar and smoke, this string is finally broke
    And a cannonball blew my eyes away"

12. As he turned away to walk, his Ma was still in shock
    At seein' the metal brace that helped him stand
    But as he turned to go, he called his mother close
    And he dropped his medals down into her hand

Only A Hobo

Words and Music by Bob Dylan

Moderate country waltz

1. As I was out walk - ing on a cor - ner one day I
2. blan - ket of news - pa - per cov - ered his head As the
3. take much of a man to see his whole life go down To

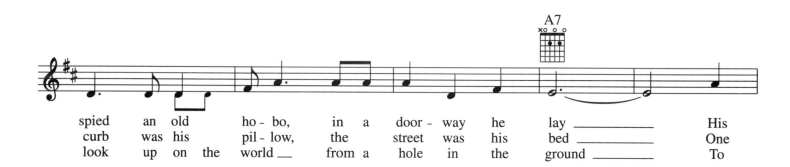

spied an old ho - bo, in a door - way he lay _____ His
curb was his pil - low, the street was his bed _____ One
look up on the world __ from a hole in the ground _____ To

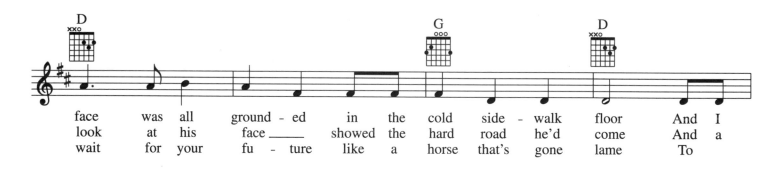

face was all ground - ed in the cold side - walk floor And I
look at his face _____ showed the hard road he'd come And a
wait for your fu - ture like a horse that's gone lame To

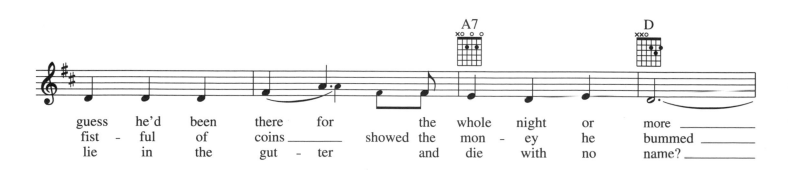

guess he'd been there for the whole night or more _____
fist - ful of coins _____ showed the mon - ey he bummed _____
lie in the gut - ter and die with no name? _____

Copyright © 1963, 1968 Warner Brothers Inc.; renewed 1991, 1996 Special Rider Music.
All Rights Reserved. International Copyright Secured.

When The Ship Comes In

Words and Music by Bob Dylan

Medium bright

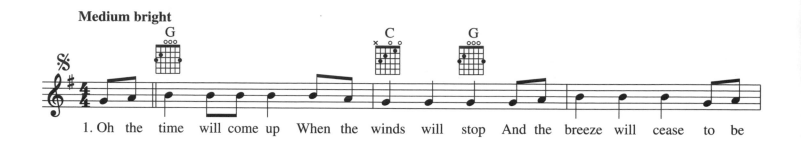

1. Oh the time will come up When the winds will stop And the breeze will cease to be

breath-in' _____ Like the still-ness in the wind 'Fore the hur-ri-cane be-gins The

ho-ur when the ship comes in Oh the seas will split And the ship will hit And the

sands on the shore-line will be shak-ing _____ Then the tide will sound And the

D.S. three times 𝄋

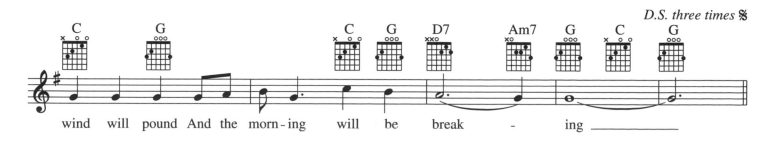

wind will pound And the morn-ing will be break - ing _____

Copyright © 1963, 1964 Warner Brothers Inc.; renewed 1991, 1992 Special Rider Music.
All Rights Reserved. International Copyright Secured.

Additional lyrics

2. Oh the fishes will laugh
   As they swim out of the path
   And the seagulls they'll be smiling
   And the rocks on the sand
   Will proudly stand
   The hour that the ship comes in

   And the words that are used
   For to get the ship confused
   Will not be understood as they're spoken
   For the chains of the sea
   Will have busted in the night
   And will be buried at the bottom of the ocean

3. A song will lift
   As the mainsail shifts
   And the boat drifts on to the shoreline
   And the sun will respect
   Every face on the deck
   The hour that the ship comes in

   Then the sands will roll
   Out a carpet of gold
   For your weary toes to be a-touchin'
   And the ship's wise men
   Will remind you once again
   That the whole wide world is watchin'

4. Oh the foes will rise
   With the sleep still in their eyes
   And they'll jerk from their beds and think they're dreamin'
   But they'll pinch themselves and squeal
   And know that it's for real
   The hour when the ship comes in

   Then they'll raise their hands
   Sayin' we'll meet all your demands
   But we'll shout from the bow your days are numbered
   And like Pharaoh's tribe
   They'll be drownded in the tide
   And like Goliath, they'll be conquered

The Times They Are A-Changin'

Words and Music by Bob Dylan

Copyright © 1963, 1964 Warner Brothers Inc.; renewed 1991, 1992 Special Rider Music.
All Rights Reserved. International Copyright Secured.

Additional lyrics

2. Come writers and critics
   Who prophesize with your pen
   And keep your eyes wide
   The chance won't come again
   And don't speak too soon
   For the wheel's still in spin
   And there's no tellin' who that it's namin'
   For the loser now will be later to win
   For the times they are a-changin'

3. Come senators, congressmen
   Please heed the call
   Don't stand in the doorway
   Don't block up the hall
   For he that gets hurt
   Will be he who has stalled
   There's a battle outside and it is ragin'
   It'll soon shake your windows and rattle your walls
   For the times they are a-changin'

4. Come mothers and fathers
   Throughout the land
   And don't criticize
   What you can't understand
   Your sons and your daughters
   Are beyond your command
   Your old road is rapidly agin'
   Please get out of the new one if you can't lend your hand
   For the times they are a-changin'

5. The line it is drawn
   The curse it is cast
   The slow one now
   Will later be fast
   As the present now
   Will later be past
   The order is rapidly fadin'
   And the first one now will later be last
   For the times they are a-changin'

Paths Of Victory

Words and Music by Bob Dylan

Moderato

Trails   of   trou - bles   Roads   of ___ bat - tles

Paths   of   vic - to - ry   { I* / We }   shall ___ walk

last time Fine

* *first time only*

1. The   trail   is   dust - y   And   my   road   it   might   be   rough   But   the

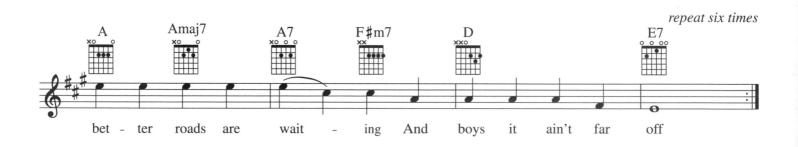

repeat six times

bet - ter   roads   are   wait - ing   And   boys   it   ain't   far   off

Copyright © 1964 Warner Brothers Inc.; renewed 1992 Special Rider Music.
All Rights Reserved. International Copyright Secured.

Additional lyrics

Refrain

2. I walked down by the river
   I turned my head up high
   I saw that silver linin'
   That was hangin' in the sky

Refrain

3. The evenin' dusk was rollin'
   I was walking down the track
   There was a one-way wind a-blowin'
   And it was blowin' at my back

Refrain

4. The gravel road is bumpy
   It's a hard road to ride
   But there's a clearer road a-waitin'
   With the cinders on the side

Refrain

5. That evening train was rollin'
   The hummin' of its wheels
   My eyes they saw a better day
   As I looked across the fields

Refrain

6. The trail is dusty
   The road it might be rough
   But the good road is a-waitin'
   And boys it ain't far off

Refrain

Guess I'm Doing Fine

Words and Music by Bob Dylan

Copyright © 1964, 1966 Warner Brothers Inc.; renewed 1992, 1994 Special Rider Music.
All Rights Reserved. International Copyright Secured.

Additional lyrics

2. And I've never had much money
   But I'm still around somehow
   No, I've never had much money
   But I'm still around somehow
   Many times I've bended
   But I ain't never yet bowed
   Hey, hey, so I guess I'm doin' fine

3. Trouble, oh trouble
   I've trouble on my mind
   Trouble, oh trouble
   Trouble on my mind
   But the trouble in the world, Lord
   Is much more bigger than mine
   Hey, hey, so I guess I'm doin' fine

4. And I never had no armies
   To jump at my command
   No, I ain't got no armies
   To jump at my command
   But I don't need no armies
   I got me one good friend
   Hey, hey, so I guess I'm doin' fine

5. I been kicked and whipped and trampled on
   I been shot at just like you
   I been kicked and whipped and trampled on
   I been shot at just like you
   But as long as the world keeps a-turnin'
   I just keep a-turnin' too
   Hey, hey, so I guess I'm doin' fine

6. Well, my road might be rocky
   The stones might cut my face
   My road it might be rocky
   The stones might cut my face
   But as some folks ain't got no road at all
   They gotta stand in the same old place
   Hey, hey, so I guess I'm doin' fine

Baby, Let Me Follow You Down

By Rev. Gary Davis, additional lyrics, title and arrangement contributed by Eric Von Schmidt and Dave Van Ronk.

Copyright © Chandos Music (ASCAP)
All Rights Reserved. International Copyright Secured.

Additional lyrics

2. Can I come home with you?
   Baby can I come home with you?
   Yes I'll do anything in this God a'mighty world
   If you jest let me come home with you

3. I'll buy you a diamond ring
   I'll buy you a wedding gown
   An' I'd do anything in this God a'mighty world
   If you jest let me follow you down

4. Baby let me follow you down
   Baby let me follow you down
   An' I'd do anything in this God a'mighty world
   If you jest let me follow you down

5. I just want you to understand
   Baby please understand
   Well, I'd do anything in this God a'mighty world
   If you just let me be your man

6. Baby let me follow you down
   Baby let me follow you down
   An' I'll do anything in this Godalmighty world
   If you jest let me follow you down

Mama, You Been On My Mind

Words and Music by Bob Dylan

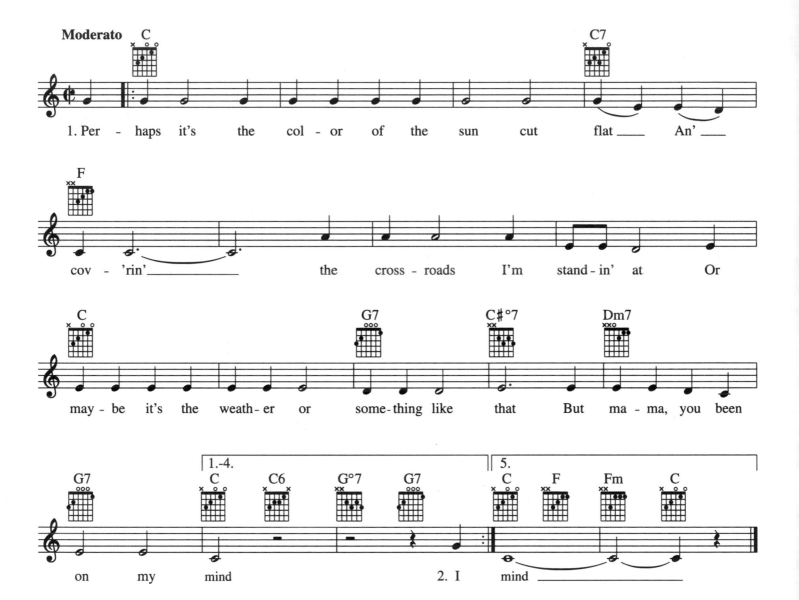

Copyright © 1964, 1967 Warner Brothers Inc.; renewed 1992, 1995 Special Rider Music.
All Rights Reserved. International Copyright Secured.

Additional lyrics

2. I don't mean trouble, please don't put me down or get upset
I am not pleadin' or sayin', "I can't forget"
I do not walk the floor bowed down an' bent, but yet
Mama, you been on my mind

3. Even though my mind is hazy an' my thoughts they might be narrow
Where you been don't bother me nor bring me down in sorrow
It don't even matter to me where you're wakin' up tomorrow
But mama, you're just on my mind

4. I am not askin' you to say words like "yes" or "no"
Please understand me, I got no place for you t' go
I'm just breathin' to myself, pretendin' not that I don't know
Mama, you been on my mind

5. When you wake up in the mornin', baby, look inside your mirror
You know I won't be next to you, you know I won't be near
I'd just be curious to know if you can see yourself as clear
As someone who has had you on his mind

I'll Keep It With Mine

Words and Music by Bob Dylan

Slow, but not draggy

1. You will search, babe, __ At an - y __ cost But how long, babe __ Can you search for what's not lost? Ev - 'ry - bod - y will help you Some peo - ple are __ ver - y __ kind __

Chorus
But if I __ can save you an - y time __ Come __ on, give it to me I'll __ keep it with __ mine __

2. I can't
3. The

Copyright © 1967 Special Rider Music, USA.
All Rights Reserved. International Copyright Secured.

Additional lyrics

2. I can't help it
   If you might think I'm odd
   If I say I'm not loving you for what you are
   But for what you're not
   Everybody will help you
   Discover what you set out to find
   But if I can save you any time
   Come on, give it to me
   I'll keep it with mine

3. The train leaves
   At half past ten
   But it'll be back tomorrow
   Same time again
   The conductor he's weary
   He's still stuck on the line
   But if I can save you any time
   Come on, give it to me
   I'll keep it with mine

Mr. Tambourine Man

Words and Music by Bob Dylan

Copyright © 1964, 1965 Warner Brothers Inc.; renewed 1992, 1993 Special Rider Music, USA.
All Rights Reserved. International Copyright Secured.

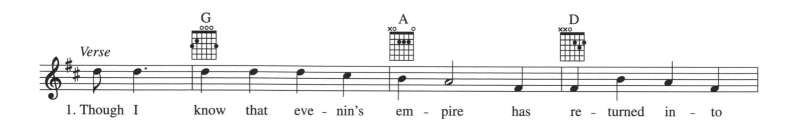

1. Though I know that eve-nin's em-pire has re-turned in-to

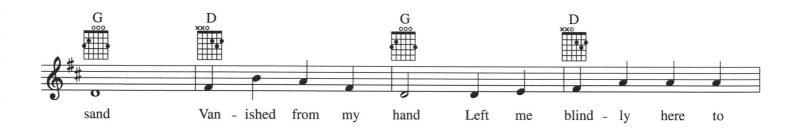

sand Van-ished from my hand Left me blind-ly here to

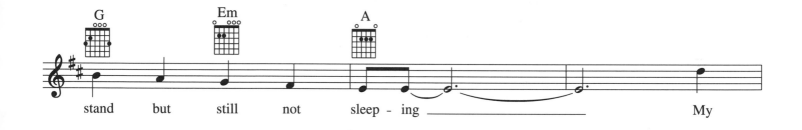

stand but still not sleep-ing _____ My

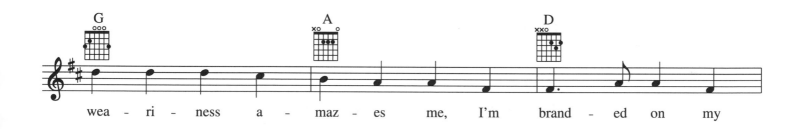

wea-ri-ness a-maz-es me, I'm brand-ed on my

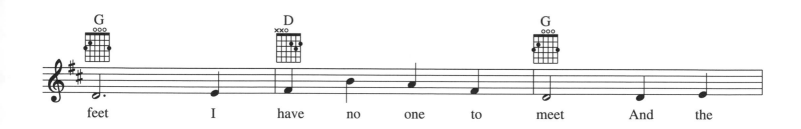

feet I have no one to meet And the

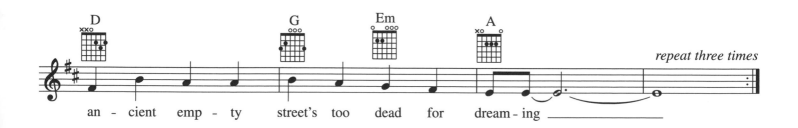

repeat three times

an-cient emp-ty street's too dead for dream-ing _____

Additional lyrics

2. Take me on a trip upon your magic swirlin' ship
   My senses have been stripped, my hands can't feel to grip
   My toes too numb to step
   Wait only for my boot heels to be wanderin'
   I'm ready to go anywhere, I'm ready for to fade
   Into my own parade, cast your dancing spell my way
   I promise to go under it

   Refrain

3. Though you might hear laughin', spinnin', swingin' madly across the sun
   It's not aimed at anyone, it's just escapin' on the run
   And but for the sky there are no fences facin'
   And if you hear vague traces of skippin' reels of rhyme
   To your tambourine in time, it's just a ragged clown behind
   I wouldn't pay it any mind
   It's just a shadow you're seein' that he's chasing

   Refrain

4. Then take me disappearin' through the smoke rings of my mind
   Down the foggy ruins of time, far past the frozen leaves
   The haunted, frightened trees, out to the windy beach
   Far from the twisted reach of crazy sorrow
   Yes, to dance beneath the diamond sky with one hand wavin' free
   Silhouetted by the sea, circled by the circus sands
   With all memory and fate driven deep beneath the waves
   Let me forget about today until tomorrow

   Refrain

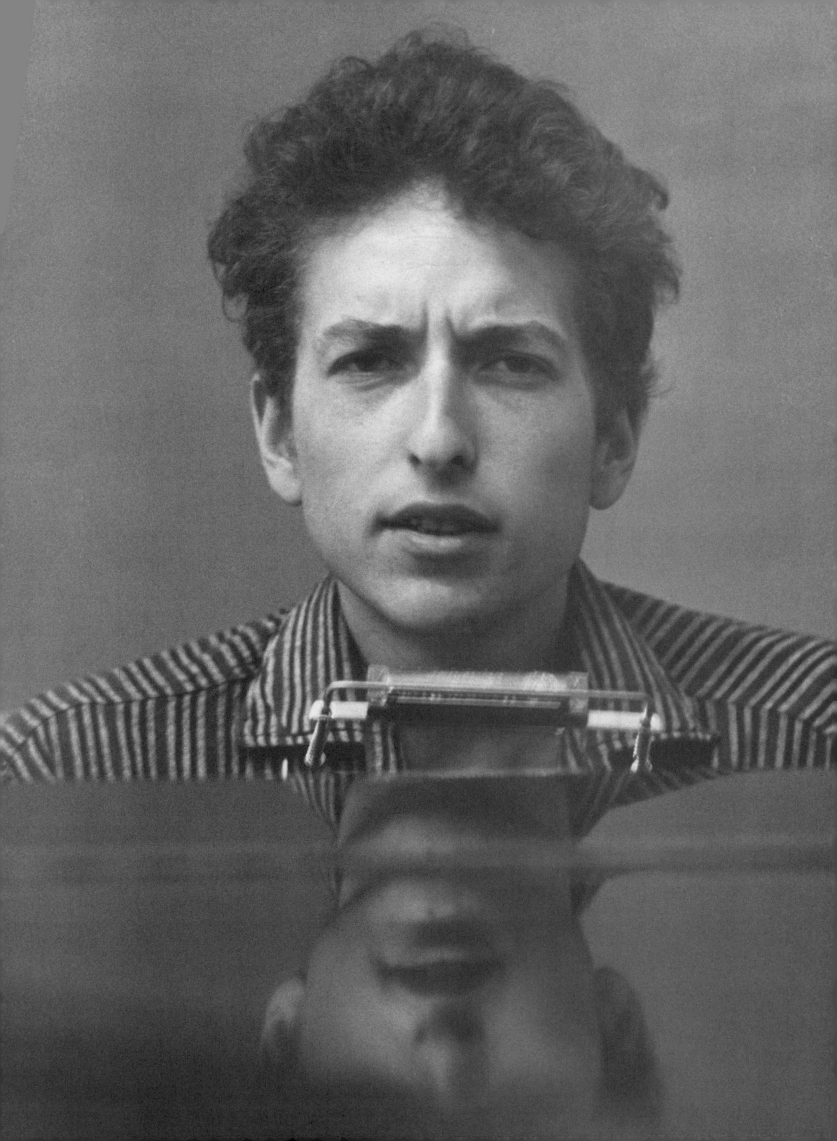